PIRATE PHOTO!

Look at the picture and complete the sentences below.

1. How many Pirates have striped hats?

2. How many Pirates have swords?

3. How many Pirates have parrots?

4. How many Pirates have eye patches?

Answers on page 95

DOT to DOT

What are the Pirates sailing in?
Join the dots and find out!

CRYPTIC CODE!

Where is the treasure?

Use the code to decipher the
directions to the buried treasure.

A B C D E F G H I J K L M N O P Q R S T U V W X Y Z
□ ∴ . ₹ X ○ ▯ ☲ △ ∩ ξ ‖ ∧ Γ ✓ + −) ☆ ⋏ · ✹ ◇ ○ N ꝯ ⟨□

−ΓX ∴○+· ✹⋏○□·◇⋏○ −▯ △−ΓX □+X
OLD BENS TREASURE of GOLD AND

⋏○∴·ξ○· ξ· ∴◇⋏ξ○X −+ ⋏○X ⋏−₹⋏ ξ·Γ□+X
RUBIES IS BURIED on RED ROCK ISLAND

The treasure is buried on _Red Rock_

AHOY!

This Pirate has spotted a message.
Can you work out what it says?

The Pirate message is _can we have some milk?_

A PIRATE PROBLEM!

Pirate Roger has lost something. Can you help him find it? I'll give you a clue... it rhymes with steady!

The Pirate has lost his _teady_

WORD SEARCH

Can you find these seven seas in the word search?

ARABIAN
~~NORTH~~
BLACK
RED
~~CARIBBEAN~~
~~MEDITERRANEAN~~
CASPIAN

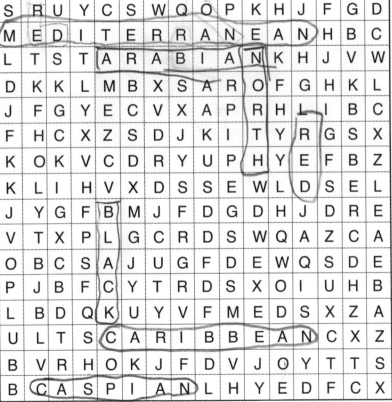

S	R	U	Y	C	S	W	Q	O	P	K	H	J	F	G	D
M	E	D	I	T	E	R	R	A	N	E	A	N	H	B	C
L	T	S	T	A	R	A	B	I	A	N	K	H	J	V	W
D	K	K	L	M	B	X	S	A	R	O	F	G	H	K	L
J	F	G	Y	E	C	V	X	A	P	R	H	L	I	B	C
F	H	C	X	Z	S	D	J	K	I	T	Y	R	G	S	X
K	O	K	V	C	D	R	Y	U	P	H	Y	E	F	B	Z
K	L	I	H	V	X	D	S	S	E	W	L	D	S	E	L
J	Y	G	F	B	M	J	F	D	G	D	H	J	D	R	E
V	T	X	P	L	G	C	R	D	S	W	Q	A	Z	C	A
O	B	C	S	A	J	U	G	F	D	E	W	Q	S	D	E
P	J	B	F	C	Y	T	R	D	S	X	O	I	U	H	B
L	B	D	Q	K	U	Y	V	F	M	E	D	S	X	Z	A
U	L	T	S	C	A	R	I	B	B	E	A	N	C	X	Z
B	V	R	H	O	K	J	F	D	V	J	O	Y	T	T	S
B	C	A	S	P	I	A	N	L	H	Y	E	D	F	C	X

(6)

Answers on page 95

TWO OF A KIND

Join the matching treasure.

ARGH!

**Barnacle Bob must walk the plank.
Connect the dots to save him.**

LOST AT SEA!

The Golden Goose must sail through the reef to reach Jamaica.

Help the ship find its way.

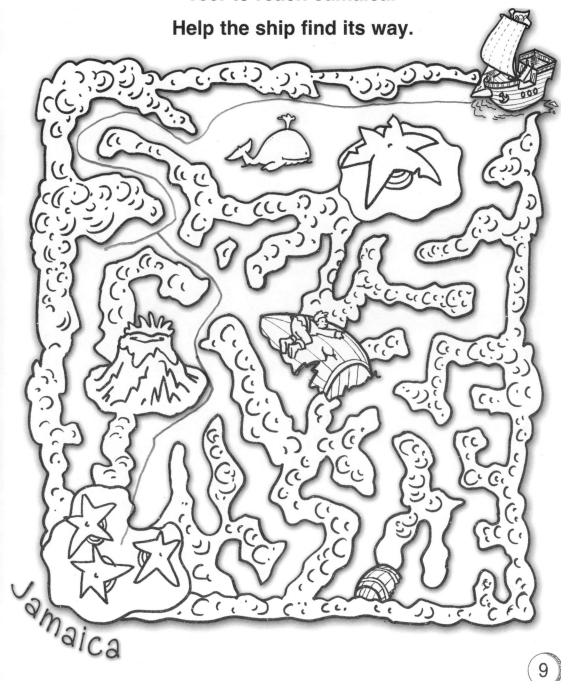

Jamaica

SPOT THE DIFFERENCE!

Can you spot the differences between these two Pirates?

How many can you find?

There are _8_ differences.

ALL TIED UP!

These Pirate Ships have all been tied together.
Write a number on the empty sails so each
line adds up to 30.

LAND HO!

The Pirates have found an island. They need a harbour, somewhere to build a camp, fresh water and food. Can you find these places on the map?

Use the icons from the box and draw them in.

FEROCIOUS FISHING!

Which Pirate has caught the shark?

COLOUR IN

Colour in the scene below.

14

MIX AND MATCH!

Can you connect the pictures to the words?
They are all parts of a Pirate Ship.

Hammock

Crow's Nest

Cannon

Anchor

Wheel

Compass

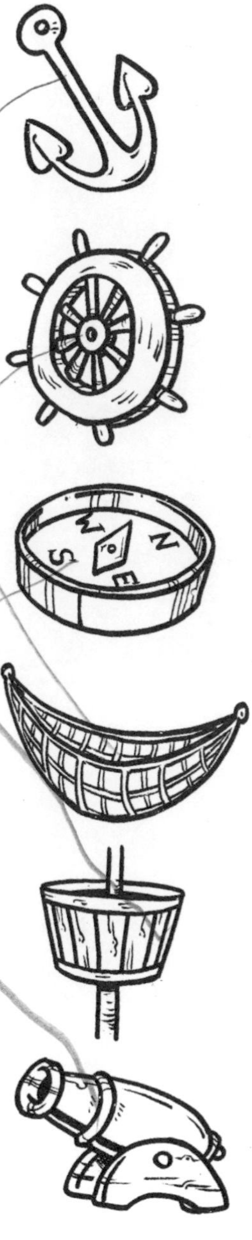

ODD ONE OUT!

Can you spot the odd one out?

1

2

3

DOT TO DOT!

What is the Island like? Join the dots to find out.
How many palm trees can you see?

There are ____ palm trees.

MUDDLING MAZE!

Find the shortest route to the treasure.
Watch out for the quicksand!

START

MONEY MATHS!

Can you work out how many gold coins are left in each bag?

Fill in the missing numbers.

27 coins, take out *5* leaves 22 coins

35 coins, take out 10 leaves *25* coins

42 coins, take out 3 leaves 39 coins

18 coins, take out *15* leaves 3 coins

FIND AND CIRCLE!

Can you find and circle all the Pirate hats in this picture?
How many hats can you find?

There are 12 **hats.**

20

CROSSWORD!

Complete the words and look at the pictures to solve the crossword. Then take the highlighted letters to complete the word below.

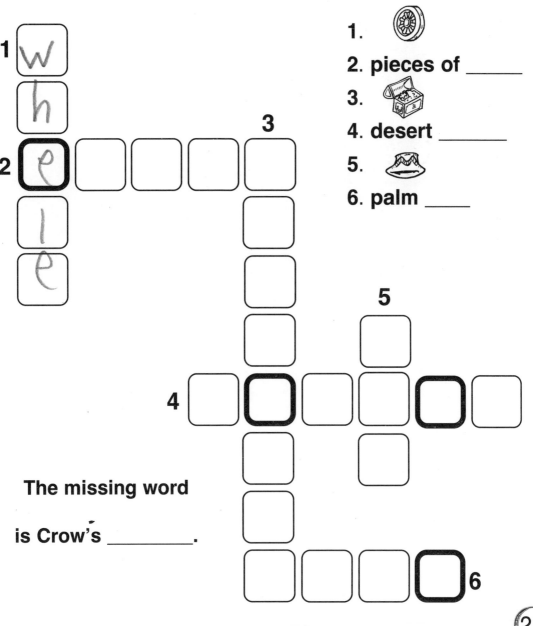

1.
2. pieces of _____
3.
4. desert _____
5.
6. palm ____

The missing word

is Crow's _____.

21

A SCURVY SPY!

**There is a spy on the Pirate ship.
Decipher the code to see who it is!**

A B C D E F G H I J K L M N O P Q R S T U V W X Y Z

Z Y X W V U T S R Q P O N M L K J I H G F E D C B A

GSV   HKB   RH   DVZIRMT   Z   HGIRKVW   SZG!

The spy is weaRINGA STRIpeD hat

(22)

HALF WAY!

Complete the picture and colour it in.

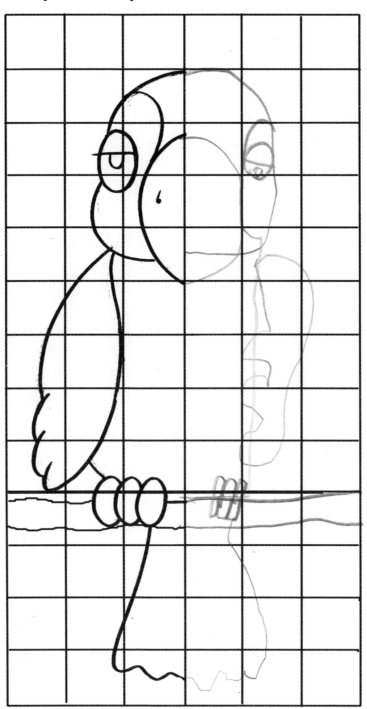

23

COUNTING FISHIES!

How many sea creatures can you see?

I can see ___ **sea creatures.**

WORD SEARCH!

Can you find these eight words?

parrot   treasure

~~map~~   hook

sword   ship

pirate   blackbeard

g	d	g	v	x	j	o	l	k	h	g	f
g	d	p	a	r	r	o	t	v	x	j	o
a	g	v	c	b	g	h	k	z	l	m	v
b	r	e	w	g	u	k	i	h	g	a	t
h	i	o	l	j	h	o	o	k	b	p	r
s	f	j	n	v	r	w	r	s	d	f	e
w	h	x	d	r	p	u	o	l	d	x	a
o	v	c	d	z	a	i	w	h	y	g	s
r	n	h	f	v	i	u	h	t	g	b	u
d	h	j	k	b	v	c	t	s	h	i	r
f	d	e	p	i	r	a	t	e	b	x	e
n	b	l	a	c	k	b	e	a	r	d	w

SHIVER ME TIMBERS!

Can you find 8 items that don't belong on the Pirate ship?

JOIN THE CREW!

Tom has packed his bags to join a Pirate Crew.
What would you take with you? Draw in the empty bags.
Remember you can take whatever you want!

HOW TO SPEAK PIRATE!

Fill in the missing letters by choosing the right vowel from the box.

a	e	i	o	u

P _ _ c _ s _ f _ _ ght

W _ lk th _ pl _ nk

Sh _ v _ r m _ t _ mb _ rs

Sw _ shb _ ckl _

_ v _ st y _

Y_ h _ ah _ y!

Cl _ mb th _ m _ zz _ n m _ st!

28

MONSTER ATTACK!

How many Pirate ships has the Giant Octopus caught? How many have two sails?

There are 9 **ships.** 3 **have two sails.**

ISLANDS, ISLANDS EVERYWHERE!

How many kinds of Islands can you find?
Remember some are the same.
Join the ones that match.

I can find ___ types of islands.

DOT TO DOT!

What is Pirate Tom sleeping on?
Join the numbers to see.

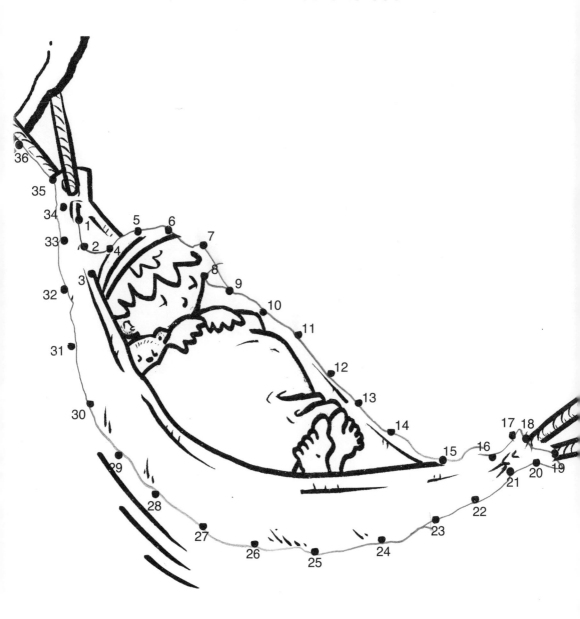

31

PIRATE SCHOOL!

Can you read what the Pirates are learning about today?

Use the code to help you!

The Pirates are learning _____.

_____

AHOY THERE!

There are three ships in sight.
Circle the one you think the Pirates should chase.

PIRATE CONFERENCE!

It's the annual Pirate conference in Hawaii!
How many ships can you see in the harbour?

There are _____ ships.

How many have a black flag?

WORD SEARCH!

Find these words in the word search.

yacht   schooner   canoe

cruiser   rowing   speed   barge

h	k	h	d	e	s	h	k	l	c	v	b
k	b	c	d	y	a	c	h	t	m	v	z
w	s	f	r	s	j	v	c	x	d	t	u
k	c	m	g	u	s	e	c	a	n	o	e
m	h	l	k	b	i	y	r	i	k	h	n
v	o	l	k	m	n	s	h	u	i	o	l
w	o	d	a	x	e	s	e	f	r	e	d
o	n	f	e	u	h	n	g	r	r	f	h
i	e	n	r	f	t	r	o	w	i	n	g
n	r	s	p	e	e	d	g	v	y	r	l
m	b	h	v	m	h	y	g	v	f	r	e
g	b	a	r	g	e	h	w	s	x	z	a

They are all types of _____.

HIDDEN NAME!

**Cross out the repeated letters
to reveal the Pirate's name.**

B C D E F G Q I M
C I L M N P Q T U
V W X Z B C D E F
T U V W X Z B C D
L M N P Q T U V W
S H A R K Y F J O
G U I L M N P Q T
W X Z B C D E G D

The Pirate's name is _____.

SPOT THE
DIFFERENCE!

Can you spot the differences between these two Pirate ships?

There are ____ differences.

MISSING HALF!

Draw in the missing half of this Pirate.
Use the boxes on the right to help you.

TRICKY TREASURE!

Help the Pirates unlock the padlocks.
Complete the sums below, by adding
the missing numbers.

9 + 8 = 17

30 − 25 = 5

10 divided by 2 = 5

10 x 6 = 60

40 + 7 = 47

What is the total?

'ORRIBLE THE OCTOPUS!

**Poor Orrible is missing some legs.
Draw them in. He should have 8.**

PIRATE PICNIC!

Pirate Ron has only got room for three of each in the Picnic boat. Cross out three of each item and write down how many are left.

| apples | 10 | coconuts | 6 | pineapples | 4 |
| loaves | 7 | ice creams | 8 | fish | 5 |

A TRICKY TREASURE RIDDLE!

Read the riddle below. Circle all the words with a in.
Then circle all the words that rhyme with day.

Sail for a day

Over the sea

And far away

Till you spy

A green palm tree

A yellow beach and

An X marking the spot!

RHYMING TIME!

Connect the words to the pictures.
Remember they must rhyme!

carrot

nail

cap

knee

seal

cat

school

goat

SAILING AWAY!

How many sails does the Golden Duck have?

The Golden Duck has ___ sails.

Now circle the largest and the smallest ones.

ODD ONES OUT!

Circle the odd ones out.

WHY?

Look at the pictures on page 45 and complete the sentences below by using the words from the word box.

Be careful some words don't belong!

A seagull is a _ _ _ _ not a fish.

A _ _ _ _ _ is _ _ _ a plant.

A _ _ _ _ _ _ _ is not an _ _ _ _ _ _ _.

---

bird	bath	boat
biscuit	not	Pirate
red	island	cup	turkey

Answers on page 96

MIRROR IMAGE

Complete the picture by drawing
in the empty squares on the right.

COLOUR IN!

Colour in Pirate Ted and his parrot.

WORDSEARCH!

Can you find these words?

bow   **mast**   **rudder**

cabin   **sail**

porthole   **stern**

t	h	g	s	d	s	c	b	n	m	i	p
h	r	d	t	c	s	a	w	q	s	d	o
l	k	b	e	h	g	c	a	b	i	n	r
k	j	o	r	g	f	r	o	i	u	j	t
n	m	w	n	j	l	j	f	c	x	s	h
m	a	s	t	g	c	d	k	j	h	i	o
a	t	f	v	g	y	j	m	k	i	u	l
s	u	g	r	u	d	d	e	r	f	g	e
t	b	v	d	x	k	j	h	g	f	d	s
m	j	k	o	i	l	p	y	h	g	t	f
g	r	t	s	a	i	l	m	g	h	f	d

UNDER ATTACK!

Help the Pirates through the maze to escape
from the Navy. They must pick up the map,
compass and water barrel first!

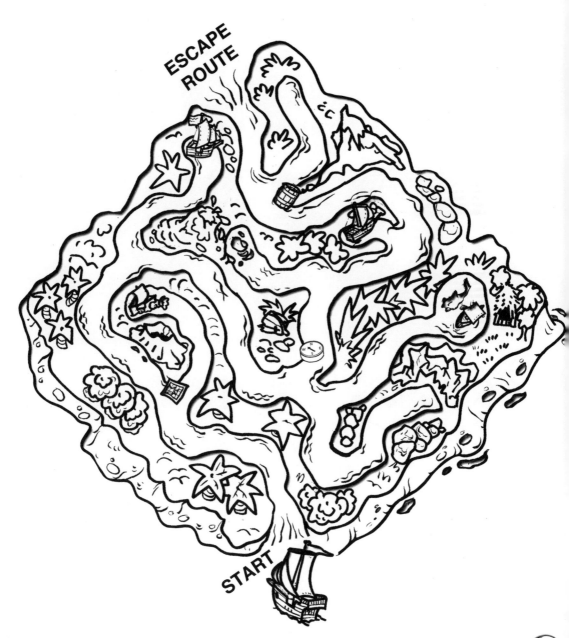

ESCAPE ROUTE

START

WORD SEARCH!

There are 6 Caribbean Islands hidden in the word search. Can you find them?

jamaica   **cuba**   **barbados**

tobago   **bahamas**   **haiti**

j	k	p	o	u	g	h	k	f	y	j	k
k	c	s	e	r	t	f	k	i	h	g	h
g	s	x	j	a	m	a	i	c	a	k	a
j	c	u	b	a	l	j	n	c	s	q	i
t	u	i	c	s	q	e	w	r	f	d	t
g	d	r	b	a	r	b	a	d	o	s	i
n	j	h	g	t	o	b	a	g	o	k	b
n	b	h	u	y	k	g	f	d	s	f	g
x	b	a	h	a	m	a	s	g	t	r	e
i	o	j	k	m	n	b	g	h	j	u	y
c	v	f	g	h	j	n	b	v	g	h	u
s	d	f	g	h	y	t	g	v	c	x	z

CAN YOU SEE?

Can you spot and circle the nine items that don't belong in this picture?

PIRATE BIRTHDAY!

It's Pirate Tom's birthday.

How many candles are on his cake?

Now draw ten more. How many candles will there be?

PIRATE CODE!

Pirate flags are used to send messages.

Read the sentences and colour in the flags.

1. A blue flag means Ahoy There!

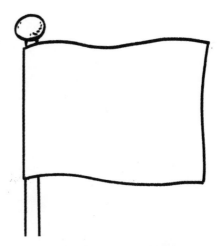

2. A red spotty flag means We've Found Treasure!

3. A black striped flag means We are near an Island.

4. A green and yellow flag means Gone for Lunch.

PIRATE FLAGS!

Pirate Bob's flag is striped.
Pirate Tom's flag has lots of triangles.

What would your flag look like?

HIDDEN TREASURE!

This Pirate has found a cave full of treasure.

What does it look like?
Draw in the treasure, remember it can be anything!

CROSSWORD!

Use the pictures to solve the crossword.

SECRET CODE.

Old Billy Blackbeard has hidden his treasure.
Can you help him write a secret code so no one finds it?

FACE NORTH   _____

WALK TEN PACES   _____

TURN LEFT   _____

WALK SIX PACES   _____

TURN RIGHT   _____

WALK ELEVEN PACES _____

THE TREASURE   _____

IS UNDER   _____

THE BANANA TREE.   _____

A B C D E F G H I J K L M N O P Q R S T U V W X Y Z

_____

DOT TO DOT!

Can you find out what this sea monster is?

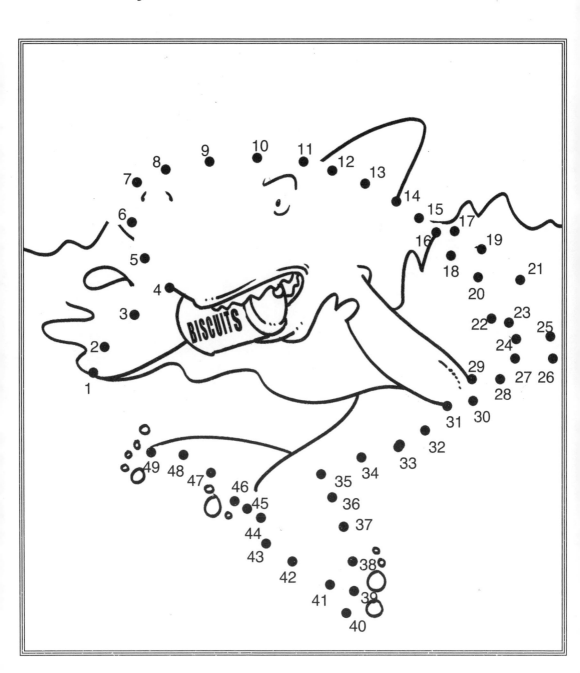

What is the sea monster eating? _____

MATCHING COINS!

Can you find the coin that matches this one?

BANANA NUMBERS!

Pirate Tom has collected some bananas for the voyage.
There should be 12 in each sack.
Draw in the missing bananas!

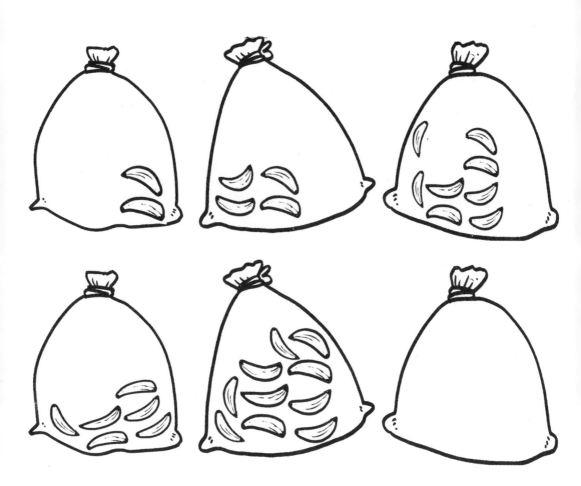

PIRATE STORY!

Write your own story underneath these pictures.
What is going on?

_____

_____

_____

PIRATE PETS!

Which pet goes with which Pirate?

WHAT IS MISSING?

Look at the picture, can you see what is missing from the bottom picture?

Draw them in.

BOOTS.

This Pirate has lost 4 pairs of boots.

Can you find them?

COLOURING IN!

Colour in each space with a dot.
What bird can you see?

WRITE YOUR OWN STORY!

Write your own story under the pictures.

1

2

_____

_____

_____

3

4

_____

_____

_____

THIRSTY!

This Pirate is very thirsty,
can you help him find the coconut juice.

ADDING FLAGS!

Colour in all the flags that add up to 24.

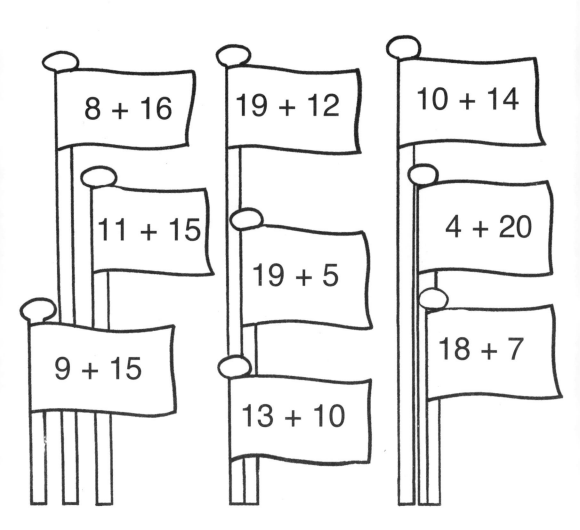

8 + 16

19 + 12

10 + 14

11 + 15

19 + 5

4 + 20

9 + 15

18 + 7

13 + 10

MONSTERS FROM THE DEEP!

How many sea monsters can you see?
Draw a line between the matching pairs.

Answers on page 96

MISSING PIECES!

**The Pirates have found a gold medallion.
Can you complete the picture?**

MONKEY BUSINESS!

The medallion has turned all the Pirates into monkeys!

**Can you unscramble the magic words
below to turn them back?**

MPJU PU NDA OWND HRTEE SIMTE

HIDDEN!

How many bananas can you find hidden in the palm tree?

There are ___ bananas.

PIRATE PICTURE!

Draw your own Pirate using the
items from the costume box.

OCEAN MAP!

Can you label the six oceans on this Pirate map?
Use the names in the word box to help you.

Pacific   North Atlantic

South Atlantic   Arctic

Antarctic   Indian

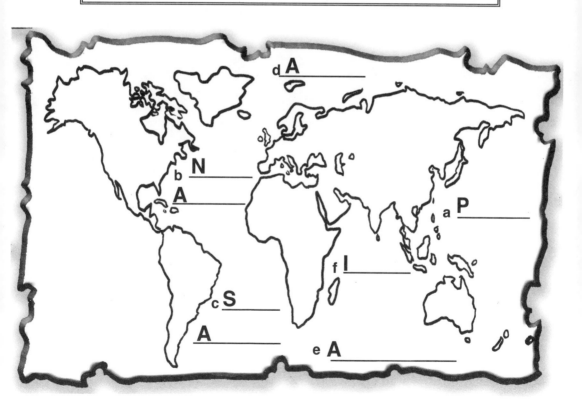

d **A** _____

b **N** _____

A _____

a **P** _____

f **I** _____

c **S** _____

A _____

e **A** _____

EYE SPY!

How many Pirates with eye patches are there?

Answers on page 96

ISLAND MAZE!

Which Island is the Pirate ship going to?

WORDSNAKE!

**How many Pirates names can you find
in the wordsnake?**

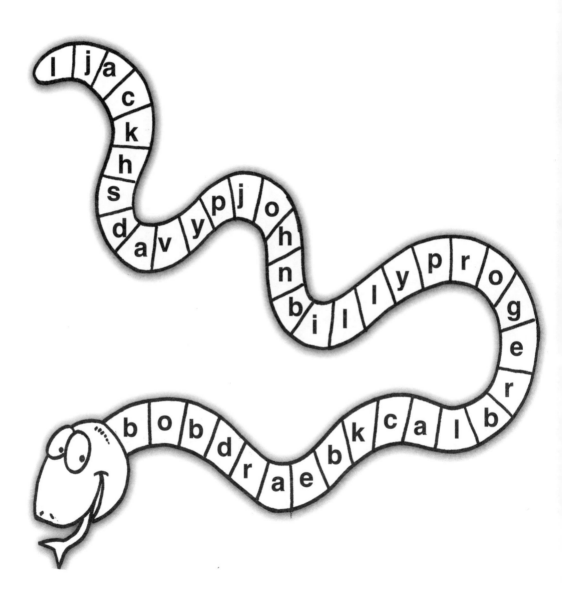

There are ___ Pirates names.

AVAST YE!

How many Pirates are rowing to the ship?

There are ___ Pirates.

DREAMING!

What is this Pirate dreaming of?

The Pirate is dreaming of _____.

TREASURE PATHS!

What is the quickest path from the beach to the buried treasure?

Path __ is the quickest.

BLACKBEARD'S BOOTS.

What kind of boots is Blackbeard wearing?
Join the dots together and colour them in.

WHERE'S POLLY?

Can you find the name of this parrot?

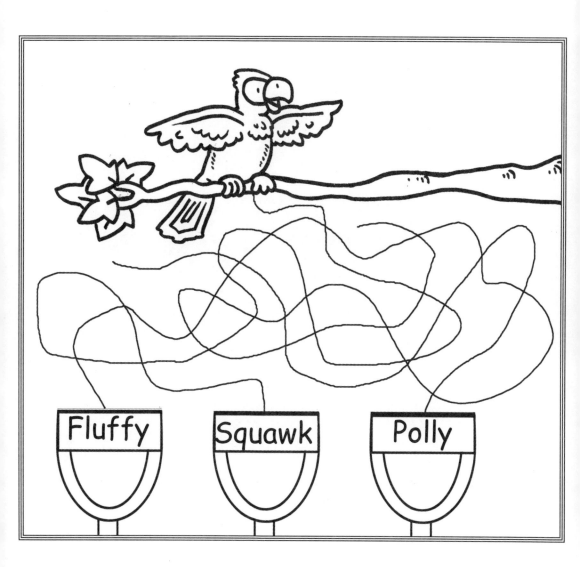

Fluffy   Squawk   Polly

The Parrot's name is _____.

WHO AM I?

Colour in these three Pirates, but read their names first!

Roger Redbeard

Billy Bluecoat

Jack Greenhat

AHOY THERE!

What can this Pirate see from the crow's nest?

The Pirate can see a _____.

ESCAPE!

A crocodile is chasing Pirate Tom but only one door is open! Help Tom choose the door that adds up to 25 so he can escape!

| 14 + 8 | 7 + 19 | 19 + 6 |
| A | B | C |

Door ___.

SPOOKY SPIRIT!

The ghost of Old Billy Whitebeard guards
his buried treasure!
You must work out the riddle to pass.

What grows on a tree,
But falls to the ground?
Is white inside,
But outside brown?

The Answer is _____.

SHIPWRECKED!

These Pirates are shipwrecked.
Choose the items from the word box that you think will
help them and draw them in.

tent	flowerpot	boat	food
crocodile	sofa	penguin	shoe
fire	television	phone	book

WORD SEARCH!

**Find these tropical island fruits
in the word search below!**

**coconut   paw paw   mango
papaya   banana
pineapple   starfruit**

a	y	i	j	v	f	a	q	w	e	r	t
k	l	c	o	c	o	n	u	t	d	w	p
o	h	g	v	b	n	h	g	f	d	s	i
i	p	a	w	p	a	w	g	u	j	b	n
l	m	c	w	u	g	a	l	b	h	g	e
b	d	q	a	w	s	m	a	n	g	o	a
i	u	h	n	k	f	v	g	r	s	x	p
q	d	r	g	y	p	a	p	a	y	a	p
b	a	n	a	n	a	t	r	e	s	z	l
p	b	q	f	e	x	u	e	g	d	f	e
k	h	v	x	f	r	y	j	k	l	o	h
v	x	s	t	a	r	f	r	u	i	t	a

SHIPS!

Captain Longbeard owns six pirate ships.
Draw in the missing ships.

Remember each ship must have the same flag.

COLOUR IN!

What name would you give this Pirate ship?
Write it on the bow and then colour the picture in.

DOT TO DOT!

Complete the dots and colour the picture in.

CROSS WORD!

Work out the words for these pictures and then complete the cross word below.

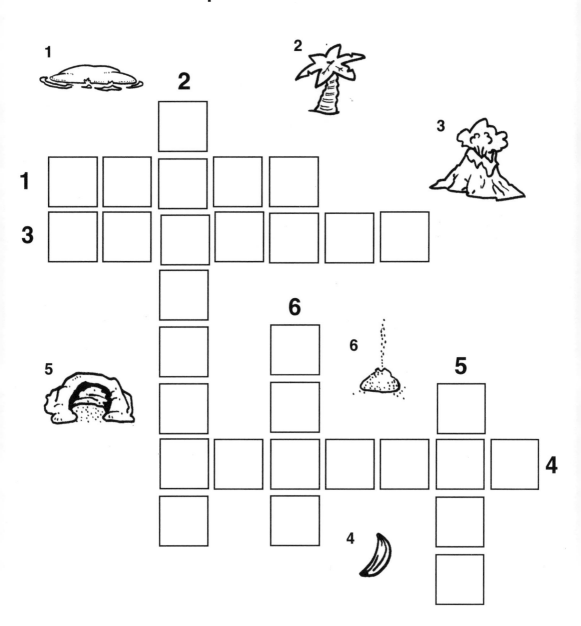

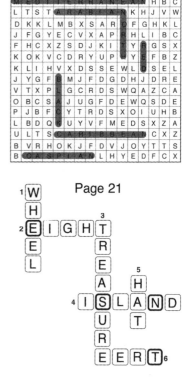

Page 1: 1. 3, 2. 4, 3. 2, 4. 2.

Page 3: Red Rock Island.

Page 4: Can we have some milk?

Page 5: Teddy.

Page 10: There are 10 differences – sword, hat, eye patch,
boots, medallion, coat, earrings, coat buttons.

Page 11: First row – 9 and 8, Second row –
5 and 8, Third row – 7, Fourth row – 12 and 5.

Page 13: The Pirate with the parrot has caught the treasure.
The Pirate with the eye patch has caught the shark.
The Pirate with the hat has caught the old boot.

Page 16: Car, walkman, kitten.

Page 17: Four palm trees.

Page 19: 1. 5, 2. 25, 3. 42, 4. 15.

Page 20: 18 hats.

Page 22: The spy is wearing a striped hat!

Page 24: 18 sea creatures.

Page 26: Items - computer, frilly lamp, toaster, phone,
electric guitar, alien, kangaroo, hoover.

Page 28: Pieces of eight, Walk the plank, Shiver me timbers,
Swashbuckle, Avast ye! Yo! Ho! Ahoy!,
Climb the mizzen mast!

Page 29: 9 ships, three have two sails.

Page 30: There are four types of islands.

Page 32: How to walk the plank.

Page 34: There are 33 ships in the harbour. 20 have black flags.

Page 35: They are all types of boat.

Page 36: Sharky Jo.

Page 37: 8 differences - number of flags, number of sails, hat,
portholes, door, anchor chain, figure head, rope.

Page 39: 9 + 8 = 17; 30 − 25 = 5; 10 divided by 2 = 5;
10 x 6 = 60; 40 + 7 = 47; Total: 134.

Page 41: 4 loaves, 7 apples, 1 pineapple, 3 coconuts,
2 fish, 5 ice creams.

Page 42: a, sail, a, day, sea, and, far, away, a, palm, a, beach,
and, an, marking, day, away, a.

Page 43: Cat/hat, goat/boat, knee/tree, school/pool, cap/map,
carrot/parrot, nail/whale, seal/wheel.

Page 44: 20 sails.

Page 21

Page 25

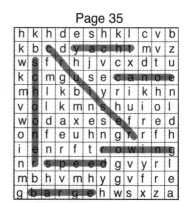

Page 35

Page 45: Odd ones out are – seagull, pirate and boat.

Page 46: A seagull is a bird not a fish. A boat is not a plant.
A pirate is not an island.

Page 52: There are two suns; a fish and a carrot in a tree;
a traffic light; a walkman; a rabbit;
a Pirate wearing a flowery hat; a plane; a camera.

Page 53: 12 + 10 = 22 candles.

Page 59: A biscuit barrel.

Page 61: Missing numbers – 10, 8, 4, 6, 2, 12.

Page 63: Pirate 1 has a goldfish, Pirate 2 has a monkey,
Pirate 3 has a lizard, Pirate four has a parrot.

Page 64: Missing - leaves from 1 palm tree; 1 parrot;
coconuts; footprints; both shovels; treasure chest.

Page 66: A parrot.

Page 69: Five flags add up to 24: 8+16; 10+14;
19+5; 4+20; 9+15.

Page 70: Ten sea monsters.

Page 72: Jump up and down three times.

Page 73: 12 bananas.

Page 75: a. Pacific; b. North Atlantic; c. South Atlantic;
d. Arctic; e. Antarctic; f. Indian.

Page 76: 4 have eye patches.

Page 77: The Pirate is going to the volcanic island.

Page 78: There are 7 Pirate names.
1, Jack 2, John, 3, Bill 4, Roger, 5, Black 6, Bear, 7, Bob

Page 79: There are 12 Pirates.

Page 80: A washing machine!

Page 81: Path C is the quickest.

Page 83: The parrot's name is Squawk.

Page 85: A whale.

Page 86: Door C.

Page 87: A coconut!

Page 51

t	h	g	e	d	s	c	b	n	m	i	p
h	r	d	t	c	s	a	w	q	s	d	o
l	k	b	e	h	g	**c**	**a**	**b**	**i**	**n**	r
k	j	o	r	g	f	r	o	i	u	j	t
n	m	w	n	j	l	j	f	c	x	s	h
m	**a**	**s**	**t**	g	c	d	k	j	h	i	o
a	t	f	v	g	y	j	m	k	i	u	l
s	u	g	**r**	**u**	**d**	**d**	**e**	**r**	f	g	e
t	b	v	d	x	k	j	h	g	f	d	s
m	j	k	o	i	l	p	y	h	g	t	f
g	r	t	**s**	**a**	**i**	**l**	m	g	h	f	d

Page 57

j	k	p	o	u	g	h	k	f	y	j	k
k	c	s	e	r	t	f	k	i	h	g	**h**
g	s	x	**j**	**a**	**m**	**a**	**i**	**c**	**a**	k	**a**
j	**c**	**u**	**b**	**a**	l	j	n	c	s	q	**i**
t	u	i	c	s	q	e	w	r	f	d	**t**
g	d	r	**b**	**a**	**r**	**b**	**a**	**d**	**o**	**s**	**i**
n	j	h	g	**t**	**o**	**b**	**a**	**g**	**o**	k	b
n	b	h	u	y	k	g	f	d	s	f	**g**
x	**b**	**a**	**h**	**a**	**m**	**a**	**s**	g	t	r	**e**
i	o	j	k	m	n	b	g	h	j	u	y
c	v	f	g	h	j	n	b	v	g	h	u
s	d	f	g	h	y	t	g	v	c	x	z

Page 57 (crossword)

1. SWORD
2. OCEAN / CROW'S NEST (ISLAND)
3. PIRATE
4. PARROT (down)
5. FLAG
6. PARROT

Page 89

a	y	i	j	v	f	a	q	w	e	r	t
k	l	**c**	**o**	**c**	**o**	**n**	**u**	**t**	d	w	**e**
o	h	g	v	b	n	h	g	f	d	s	**s**
i	**p**	**a**	**w**	**p**	**a**	**w**	g	u	j	b	**n**
l	m	c	w	u	g	a	l	b	h	g	**e**
b	d	q	a	w	s	**m**	**a**	**n**	**g**	**o**	**a**
i	u	h	n	k	f	v	g	r	s	x	**p**
q	d	r	g	y	**p**	**a**	**p**	**a**	**y**	**a**	**p**
b	**a**	**n**	**a**	**n**	**a**	t	r	e	s	z	**l**
p	b	q	f	e	x	u	e	g	d	f	**e**
k	h	v	x	f	r	y	j	k	l	o	h
v	x	**s**	**t**	**a**	**r**	**f**	**r**	**u**	**i**	**t**	a

Page 93

1. BEACH
2. PALM TREE
3. VOLCANO
4. BANANA
5. CAVE
6. SAND